Dry Heat

Light & Life on an Arizona Army Post

Tom Decker (signature)

Tom Decker

authorHOUSE®

AuthorHouse™
1663 Liberty Drive
Bloomington, IN 47403
www.authorhouse.com
Phone: 1-800-839-8640

© 2010 Tom Decker. All rights reserved.

No part of this book may be reproduced, stored in a retrieval system, or transmitted by any means without the written permission of the author.

First published by AuthorHouse 6/9/2010

ISBN: 978-1-4490-7475-3 (e)
ISBN: 978-1-4490-7474-6 (sc)

Library of Congress Control Number: 2010907664

Printed in the United States of America
Bloomington, Indiana

This book is printed on acid-free paper.

For
Kylie, Maia, Samuel, and Maxwell,
that they know the meaning of
Hua!

Dry Heat

An Introduction

Chaplains and soldiers…

Army Chaplains have played an important role in the history of the United States military since America's Continental Congress first chartered its inception two weeks after the birth of the Army itself on June 29, 1775. The chaplains have always closely identified with the life and lot of soldiers, as part and parcel of the Army's mission. Chaplains and chaplain assistants still rise early to run PT and train with soldiers in the heat and cold. They listen to their troubles and sometimes are asked to intercede with leaders, subordinates, or with an angry spouse. Chaplains perform and mend marriages; they bless and instruct children. Sometimes they even preside over the end of relationships gone awry. They counsel family and career moves of soldiers. They conduct religious services according to the dictates of their own religious affiliation and yet they see to it that special groups with special needs are able to meet their own religious requirements. Soldiers ask and expect chaplains to pray with and for them. Soldiers sometimes expect sympathy but they respect moral, physical, and emotional strength. Chaplains comfort the sick and wounded. Unit ministry teams work together to prevent suicides. Chaplains bury the dead, and stand with soldiers and families when final taps are played and America's flag is folded. Additionally chaplains, chaplain assistants, and each unit ministry team works the never-ending administrative details of today's modern military: budgets and the constant fight for space and manpower allotments on the installation. During my time as Staff Chaplain, (1996-2000), the orders came to demolish the last remaining World War II *wood*, "temporary" wooden structures built to support the World War II buildup. Down came the Rowdy Street Chapel, a fitting name for a soldiers' chapel in an old cantonment area! A short time later the post constructed a new multi-use chapel facility in the Military Intelligence School area.

…on a high desert post

The beautiful and historical setting for Fort Huachuca, at the mouth of Huachuca Canyon, is an important part of the soldier's and family's experience at the almost mile high installation. When World War II Medal of Honor Recipient 2LT Vernon Baker spoke at a parade ground ceremony honoring all the WWII African American recipients of the medal, he said that he owed his life to the hard training he received on the hills and canyons of the high-desert mountainous post. The names of the installation's landmarks and terrain features are soldiers' names: Laundry Ridge, Bonnie Blink, "the post cemetery," Reservoir Hill, Apache Flats, Grierson Avenue, Carter Street, Soldiers'

Chapel, Hangman's Warehouse, the Buffalo Corral, Cavalry Barracks, and so on. The post's environment is full of wild life—especially after dark—that includes deer, bob cats, coyotes, groups of javelina—small, wild pig- like animals—coatimundi, desert foxes, raccoons, possums, skunks, and desert hares. When the occasional errant bear or cougar is captured, it is relocated to a safer more remote area. The post has its working dogs and horses, and as the nation's concern for the environment grows, the protection of the post's natural resources becomes an ever increasing concern to commanders and the post's residents.

Poetry's window

Poetry opens a small window into the life of an event, a person's thoughts or feelings, a time, or a space. The poems, here set down on paper, captured some of the people and activities when I was privileged to serve as "post chaplain." Since that time was shortly before the infamous 9-ll Attack on America, the post's training schedule was routine for Military Intelligence and Signal soldiers. At the time, the training might have appeared boring to an outsider or even irrelevant to a new soldier, but in war time the skills and Army Values instilled on that desert post become critical to the nation's defense. Since the desert environment has long been favored for signal and communication innovations, the post concurrently and quietly carried on research and development for strategic and defense activities. Always ready when the Army called, the post deployed soldiers for training and sometimes for combat support in far-flung places.

Fort Huachuca had three dedicated chapels and about 15 chaplains and the same number of chaplain assistants and a few civilians on its "unit ministry team." The writing of these few poems occurred over a span of time when I was employed with the day-to-day activities within the installation chaplain's office; not surprisingly then, the chaplain's own interior life reflected on the day to day life of colleagues, chaplains, assistants, soldiers, wildlife, and the surrounding area. The connection between one's God—and truth be told, *gods*—and his/her work is strong and cannot be denied. Someone has said something to the effect that all poetry—sooner or later—is about love. Love of God is the ultimate, but we usually work out our loves in our families, offices, cubicles, and associations with colleagues, friends, lovers, and acquaintances. Carol Nuebling-Ney is an artist acquaintance and a friend from the neighboring city of Sierra Vista. She graciously provided the pen and ink drawings for this book. Colonel Ted Chopin, Garrison Commander during my time at Huachuca, called prideful attention to the fact that the Army's famous *"Hua"* undoubtedly was a derivative from Fort Huachuca, often called Fort *Hua* by the soldiers who lived and worked there. The cover photograph was taken by the author at one of the many ceremonies that marked significant transitions in the life of the installation.

The Army Quarters where we lived at 151B Grierson Avenue were not air-conditioned as were none of the historical homes on that street. The earliest homes were built of adobe, and due to the thickness of the walls, did not need air conditioning, contrary to what people believe about Arizona's summer temps. The later homes—ours was built in 1912—had more than ample window coverage which allowed for shutting out the heat or allowing the cool breezes of Huachuca Canyon to flow through the houses in the evenings. Unbelievably, we never missed the air conditioning, but then the heat in Arizona is "dry heat."

The poems "Bread of Life," "Show the Colors," and "Standing Invitation" were formerly printed in *The Lutheran Forum*. The poem "Salvation Beat" was printed in Fort Huachuca's newspaper *The Scout*. The poem "The Name's Chopin" was read at the colonel's farewell.

Hua!

Tom Decker
Signal Hill, California
2010

Contents

You gotta get up	1
Heaven	2
Monsoons might be early this year	3
The Water Nazi	4
Reptilian	5
Watch your step, especially in the dark	7
Rest in Peace	8
Alibi round	9
Veterans	11
Tracked by time	12
Government work	13
No rocket scientist	14
Haberdasher of Tombstone	15
Lynda's Barber Shop	16
Army housing	19
Close quarters	20
The shower	21
Disarming Abernathy	22
Pleasantries of the evening	24
Highwater	27
Border crossing	29
Show the colors	30
Standing invitation	31
Pilgrims	33

WWJD	35
Rest top	36
Mystery of the kingdom	37
Finding religion	38
The next town over	40
The name's Chopin	43
Bulletins I, Eschaton	46
Bulletins II, Semper fi	48
Bulletins, III. When beads count	49
Bulletin, IV. Evangel of the world	50
This guy	51
The Intervention Rag	52
The salvation beat!	58
The bread of life	62
Big Appetite	63
Sometimes	64
Chapter 9	65
Sunnive and Jon	67
Sunnive and Jon II	68
Baseball's Opener	69
No black eye for America	71
Dry heat	73
Keepers of the Spirit	74
You are sleeping	75
A Prayer for the Army's BirthdayJune 14 1775	76

You gotta get up

Assembly sounds at 0555 down on
Apache Flats and everybody stands
at ease to face the flag pole which the

darkness hides so we listen for the cannon
and the piped-in bugle plays reveille and
the soldiers all go to present arms which
    means that

America's Army has begun another day.

Heaven

is the farthest
thing from anybody's mind
as the car lights on I-10
peek down Texas Canyon

and not one of them thinks
one whit about a bunch
of soldiers preparing to salute the flag
and do a battalion run

all before breakfast.
The battalion commander
sent an email to say
that a couple of chaplain assistants

were real studs because they
carried the colors up
Laundry Ridge and down again.
The communion of saints is

a funny thing
to contemplate.
And this is
as good as it gets.

Monsoons might be early this year

The rest
of the country
celebrated Spring's
floods on the evening news
--wet--
while Arizona
wonders if the dry
heat will finally win as
arroyos chiseled in stone
wait the summer's
blue black clouds.

On a
good day,
the rain comes
in a steady downpour
that overflows roof lines
and flushes gutters to grace
salvia and petunias which up to now
had only known hand watering against the
    creeping desert.

This gusher
floods dry washes,
making them dangerous
to cross, but it's all right
since folks'll get by for one more year
now that the rains have come, but
the monsoons will not make the evening
    news.

The Water Nazi

The Command Sergeant Major
on patrol for national interest,
prowls the post's streets and alleys
listening, listening, listening
for the tell-tale tick, tick, tick
of a midnight water sprinkler.

The price of green lawns
on this Army installation
is a nasty gram, courteous but succinct,
noting dutifully the post's policy on watering:
Saturdays and Tuesdays between 6 and 8
    pm.

Lush flower beds and green lawns,
bountiful vegetation, beautiful to behold,
verdant evidence of caring
    homeowners and proud gardeners;
silent testimony
    against nocturnal transgressors of post
    policy
that allows all the water you want but only "if
    the hose is hand held."

Monsoons make honest folks out of
people who just want some green grass.

Reptilian

In
the dark,
while Orion
watches, one
snake reaches

out to another,
maybe six feet;
in the dark
even more.

Trails and tails
cross the road
not bothering
to wait

for cars.
Rattlers,
these predawn
tattlers of what

it takes
to keep
the desert
at bay

in the dark,
proving,
I suppose,
that God truly

has a sense
of design
if not
humor.

Watch your step, especially in the dark

Looking for snakes, an old habit left over from
    my youth on the banks of the Last Chance
    Ditch
where garter snakes lay on the banks and
    slipped
into the water as they sensed your presence,

now I walk the dog, one eye peeled,
even after dark when loose snakes of the
    desert
hunt under the moon, and slip into the night
not unlike me as I round the last hill

with no lights behind the house,
thinking that I know
where they're apt to lie--even in the dark.
Our paths seldom cross .

Is it luck or that I watch
where I walk?
I never know for sure,
and the snakes don't talk.

Rest in Peace

We
want
to bury
him in this
here 40 mm
shell casing, he
was in the Marines
first, and then the Army,
not that it makes any difference,
but we think he'd like that.

Alibi round

Can you
believe that
this family had
their friend's ashes
packed into a dummy
hand grenade? Least I
think it was a dummy. Well
the cemetery guy he didn't bat
an eye, just dug it out a bit more
there in the bottom of the hole and
set that grenade pretty as you'd please.
Another veteran gone to his eternal reward.

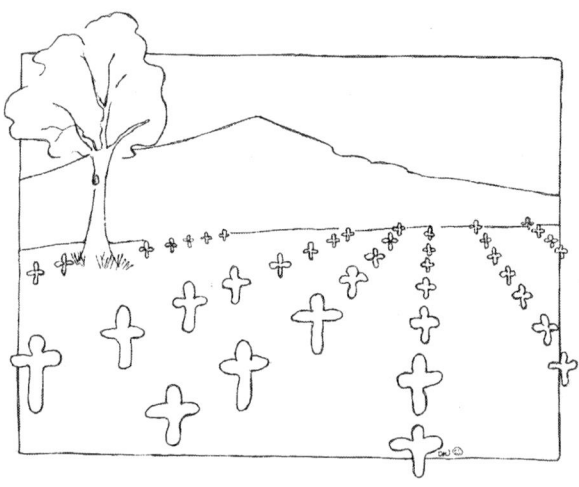

Veterans

It's nine
funerals now
in as many days, and
they want a chaplain to go.
Protestant or Catholic? Well,
Protestant or was he Methodist? Guess it
don't matter now does it? He didn't go to
    church
much anyway, and the family, well, they just
want somebody to pray when they fold
the flag. We hear that there's a real
nice honor guard that fires a volley
and folds the flag. He would
have liked that. He was in
the Army, you know.
World War II. The
service is at one,
can somebody
be there?

Tracked by time

Orion stalks across the sky, steps
over the desert blooms and
owns the night except
for the skunk that
runs beneath the
house as I come
down the
walk.

Government work

Just a few pictures from home
scotch taped between my in and out box,
checked at least twice a day to remind me
    why I work.

No rocket scientist

Orion doesn't hunt,
Peliades ain't no virgin,
anyway she went south
with Heliades while
Sirius skipped town
with Major the
dog, but the
moon is
blue.

Haberdasher of Tombstone

hey, cowboy!

you there,
with the giddy-up branding iron
at the old corral waiting
for the boot hill
bar mitzvah!

we missed ol' bat & wyatt
slapping leather at the ok corral,
but helldorado days
are a sure thing, so
shalom, til next
year and we'll
saddle up at old tombstone.

Lynda's Barber Shop

So how do you want your hair cut today,
    colonel?
Oh, forgive me, I forgot, you want to be called
    chaplain!
Can you forgive me? Please? Just a little off
    the top,
and on the sides too? Okay, that I can do.

Hey, watch that line on that Marine's head,
He just wants it close, high and tight is what
    he said.
Hold the clippers like this, and you'll get the
    idea,
Hey, dude, hope you don't mind, but we want
    you lookin' good
when you leave here.

I'd never be a good teacher, too impatient.
But I want to give everybody a chance.
We all got to have a chance. Don't you
    believe that, sir?
Being a chaplain and all? God gives us all a
    chance.

Hello, this is the barber shop.
Yeah, I'm here, but I don't want to talk to you,
And if you don't stop calling me, I'll never
    speak
With you again! You got that straight?

Did I tell you the latest about the wedding?
You don't want to know what I found out about
 that guy.
How come it is that they never tell you the
 whole story up front,
and then you have to find out the hard way?

We're going to get another chair in here?
Remember Jose, well, we're getting his chair
 back in here.
Poor Jose, he never deserved what he got.
I couldn't believe it when they told me.

You want to check the hair cut, colonel?
Sorry I mean chaplain! Sir! Hey, you didn't
 look!
I ought to swipe you with the mirror for that!
I take pride in what I do in here!
I give good hair cuts, I do.

I just love these soldiers.
They're really good people. They are.
Except for that nut who calls me here all the
 time.
Hey, guy, how's that for a hair cut?

Army housing

We live in a national register house of sorts
across from the museum which was once
a club for sergeants,
and then a bachelor officers' quarters,

and even a rifle rest for an MP
taking aim at a murderous fugitive
even, by God, a chapel of sorts,
and now the snowbirds come '

to look at the petrified buffalo soldiers
from before the time
when they closed the post
after the big war,

and the folks look at our house
and wonder
if it's open
for tours.

Dry Heat

Close quarters

Some mornings
I hear the neighbor's
kids through the thin US
Army walls, morning talk.
Boys will be boys even in their
prattling yammer, and I wonder
if God listens to folks all over the
world jabbering like five year
olds waking up in the same
room with our brother with
the murmur of small talk
and whatever it is that
brothers tell brothers
with the sleep still
in our eyes.

The shower

My
wife
says that
she needs help
to take her shower,
and so I start the water,
and test it to see if it's too
hot, and I tell her it's okay,
but she insists on testing it
too, and then I help her slip her
nightgown over her head and
she starts to cry and when
I ask her what's
wrong, she says
that she's
scared.

Disarming Abernathy
(Grierson Avenue in the '30s)

This woman hadn't been here since she was 9;
she's now over 70 so she left here
in the late 30s which was even before
World War II, and she wanted to see the
    house

where she grew up all at once one summer
    day
when a Sergeant, Abernathy by name,
    rang the bell
and shot her dad at the front door
    and then her mother
as she came down the stairs
    to see who came to call.

The sergeant went from house
    to house to see who would
answer the door so he could
    let the officer corps and
the whole damned Army
    know that he wouldn't take it anymore.
The sergeant rang up four dead
    before the MPs

got him behind the post chaplain's house,
and the score ended four for the sergeant
and one for the Army
but the Army won in the end.

The old woman said that the one thing
    she still remembered
was her mother's braided hair
    slowly coming undone
as she fell down the front stairs,
and from what she could remember
not much has changed
    on Grierson Avenue.

Pleasantries of the evening

Evening
walks the dog,
a simple routine
to sniff the night
and check who's marked
this territory and know that
they've left the neighborhood.

Families
do what needs
to be done to keep
house and home together
a hero's part of the nation's
army, going about its silent business.

Quiet
marshals her
vigilance to watch
over swing sets and
driveways so the world
can be held off one more day.

Colonels
work late, and
this one's probably
been at it since six, tending
the Army's business. Glad to be
home now to smooth the wrinkles out.

Wives
wait their
husbands' return
and when the kids have
gone to bed, and she wonders
if tomorrow will be the same and
sighs knowing that nothing changes.

Kids
grow up
in the nation's
army, and know well
the rhythm of the night
with its silent yards and kitchens.

Highwater

the
tsunami
rolled in about ten
or so, and nobody saw
it coming, least of all

buck & laney,
who said they were
going to tucson for the day,
just leaving when the first wave

raced
through the
house, breakers
crashing against the walls,
soaking memories and pictures.

the waves
crested and ran
through the living
room, the dining room

and kitchen, out the back
porch, and down the ramp,
and before we knew it, the upstairs
bedrooms were swallowed up,
and we were
   Drowning,
      Drowning,
         Drowning.

the dog
and the cat
almost floated away
but swam to a passing pillow,
and were just drying off when

buck & laney
walked by the debris,
flotsam of the gigantic wave,
and wondered if it was going to cool off,
now that the monsoons had come,

it'd been
a nice afternoon,
they said, as they
disappeared into the house. #

Border crossing

Was he looking for a ride,
coming out of the shadows?
A coyote on the hillside
just above Grierson Pool
on officer's row?

No habla Español,
and he didn't bother to show
me the pictures of his wife and kids
as he vanished into the night

along with the other 70,000
or so Mexicans who came
across the border last month.
But he hadn't been caught yet.

Show the colors

This morning
at church the pastor
dedicated two flags, both
red, white and blue 'cause this is
America, and we want to be sure of
who we are and what we stand for, but
when everybody went up to the altar for
communion I decided that we could do with
a good picture of the Host himself up close
and in color, unedited and previously
unpublished, along with some of the
more famous guests who had made
it big as far as sainthood goes and
who cheer the rest of us on, but
I'm not sure that the guests
would like it, probably
too uppity, and not
patriotic enough,
but that's what
this church
needs.

Standing invitation

He anastasis, in Greek, or the descent into hell,
and the thing I like is that Jesus moves out
like he knows what he's doing, walks
over the doors of hell without so
much as bothering to knock
and extends a hand to a
dead Adam and Eve,
when nobody
wants to
give so
much as a
hand to some
Tucson panhandler
with his hand out and
you don't want to get involved,
and old Adam and Eve don't know
what to say, and the rest of the saints
just stand there open-mouthed dumb, and
I told Jan that He really extends a hand to all
of us, and she said, that she really liked that in
    Jesus.

Pilgrims

come to see
what the black coats
built just south of tucson,
on the santa cruz river, smooth
adobe walls of the white dove of the desert.

So how
close can we
park asks my wife
as we cruise the front
row of winter visitors' cars

and pickups
and walk ever so
slowly into the coolness
of the dove's frescoed walls

to take
a seat with the
saints and angels
who watch the curious
procession of cameras, halter tops
and straw hats.

We sit
in the back
to make it easy for
my wife with her new
blue cane, self-conscious
of what it implies, not expecting
any healing here,

So when
it's time to go,
I drive right up to
the front door of the white
dove so she won't have so far to walk.

Other pilgrims
have been here before us.

WWJD

The Yaquis sell fry bread and the sign
says Indian tacos which the fat man
politely explains for first time visitors,
and he smiles and says okay, and one

of the fat women, maybe his wife, begins
to pat a tortilla while the other lays a
shell in hot fat which bubbles on a small
gas grill and the fat man rolls out another

dough roll from the plastic bag which keeps
the flies off. We stay in our car because it's
easier that way, and we eat the tortillas
in the shade of a ramada and then
we drive back to Ft Huachuca.

Rest top

When it's time to go, I check out
the men's room appropriately tiled
in browns and blue mostly for the tourists
who want a little relief from the drive

from Tucson. The restroom looks
like it was done just last year,
and I did notice that the Santa Cruz
was dry this time of year.

Mystery of the kingdom

Saturday we drive to Tombstone
just to get out of Dodge,
and the ok corral is still okay
so we go on to St David's,

which is a small Mormon settlement
where there's a Catholic monastery
and nobody knows for sure how Mormons
and Catholics get along

and we don't stop for long
because we want to look at the ducks
on the small Mormon lake
but the gate guard won't let us in

because we're not members
and so we smile at the gate
and turn the car around and drive on to
    Benson,
and Jan says, What's the next town?

Finding religion

I have to admit to these guys that I'm lost
and they looked at each other, as if to say well
we know where we're at, because it's
    Saturday
and we're leaning up against this pickup truck
    in Benson

so I ask them if they know where the Lutheran
    Church is,
and they all look at each other and then one
    guy says
you drove past it back on the highway, and
    another guy
says nah that's the Methodist Church, and
    they both

scratch their heads and look at each other,
    and one guy
says well I should know because I'm a
    Lutheran and
was married in a Lutheran Church but it didn't
    work
because I got divorced in the Municipal Court,

and then one of them says I think it's up by
    the school
so you go up this street and turn left and
    follow to where the road forks and then
    one of them says nah it ain't on that street,

and two of them agree that I should follow
   them and they'd

go check it out to see just what the hell the
   address
is anyway, so we followed them for about two
   blocks and they
unlocked the thrift store and dug out the local
   Benson Gazette
or whatever, and found the church page, and
   they said,

well it's on 6th and Gila, (the skinny one
   pronounces
it GEE-la, and the other one says, no it's
   pronounced HEE-la,
and the skinny one said GEE-la, and his
   partner rejoins,
nah, it's HEE-la, okay, CHEE-la

and the other one said, Jeez, and then let it
   go thinking
I suppose, that you can only do so much with
   somebody
who's hardheaded or just don't want to learn.
Anyway, it's not far from here, and we'll show
   you

where to go, and that's how we found
Peace in the Valley Lutheran Church
in Benson, Arizona.

The next town over

was Wilcox and
and I told my wife
that if we had a cell phone
we could just call Arlo and
Ophelia and meet them at the
Desert Pony in Elfrida
which seemed like a good thing
to do, at any rate better
than going to Wilcox again,
so we pulled over to Stuckey's
and I went in to use the phone
and Charles at the counter
tells me that he used to
be a chaplain's assistant
in the U. S. Air Force and
he finally had to get out
because of an accident
which left him injured,
and he got out on a medical,
and when he left the Air Force
he had to join the Catholic
Church even though he was
not Catholic at the time
but it was his salvation
because he needed the discipline
which the Air Force had given him
and he no longer had it

because he was no longer
in the service.
He said he was still Catholic
and had even married.
He didn't tell me if he
still needed the order
in his life,
and I did
not ask.

The name's Chopin

The names' Chopin, that's *Show*-pan.
You learn to pronounce mine just like you
    want me to know yours,
and everything'll be all right!
    Tina's my wife;
she's part of this too and knows the routine,
    and yes, we love this post.

The name's Chopin!
You all know how to spell HUA?
Well a lot of folks think they know,
but we here at Fort Hua-chuca
really know, so when I say
how do you spell HUA?
You all come back H-U-A!

Hua!

The names' Chopin,
and we're going to use APIC,
that's spelled A-P-I-C in case you don't know,
and we'll put Ft Huachuca ahead of the rest of
    the Army
and in the end you'll be glad rather than sad.

Hua!

The name's Chopin, so
bring on the air show,
the Dog Days of Summer,
the environmental owls,
and all lovers of phone poles,
and we'll save every drop of water
    for the thirsty San Pedro,
and win the infrastructure war at the same
    time!

Hua!

Or the name's not Chopin:
Colonel Ted, one each,
with a light coat of oil,
standing tall, fully qualified,
Army Aviator, not too dumb
to lend intelligence to what's otherwise
a medium smart corps of the Army,
only half growed
and never curried below the knees,
keeps his boots polished
even on Sunday, if you please.

Hua!

The name's Chopin.
Driven hard at Ft Hua-Chuca.
So, how do you spell Hua? That's H-U-A!

And the name's Chopin,
Colonel Ted, if you please!
And you can print that in

...*The Scout!*

Hua!

Bulletins I, Eschaton

Bulletins,
unite the church!
Omnipresent and omnipotent
Folded Energy of the parish!

Stapled presence!
Litany of the ages!
Announcer of hymns and readers!

Mighty Madonna of the minuscule!
Usher of all that is to be!

Herald of aids and circles!
Choir of the disconcerted!

Divine poop sheet!
Save us, O Lord for we
have a program.

Pastor's pumped up patter.
Padre's pigeon stew.

And parish potpourri of
potlucks and picnics.

Teachers needed
for bible school.

Vacations optional.
Minimal help with

eternal rewards.
Heaven help us
pray for a sign that
we're getting it
together.

The choir meets on
Wednesday nights; thankful

to have a reliable guide
to the peripheral
trivia of the faith.

Okay, a road map of sorts,
and it doesn't much matter
when people pitch 'em
for Christ's sake
as they
    leave for
        brunch.

Bulletins II, Semper fi

Well, somebody's got
to do it! It is, after all,
an act of charity towards
our fellow human being.
A service, of sorts. It's
scary, but nobody trains
to fold bulletins anymore, not
at the US Army Chaplain Center
and School nor is it on any
seminary curriculum,
cause everybody seems to know
how it's done.
Why, church
secretary's do it,
chaplains' assistants do it,
even some chaplains have been known
to crease a bulletin or two
when nobody else was around.
My friend says that the USMC
always had a machine
which did a pretty
good job every time
they needed
a bulletin.
Which proves
you can
depend
on the
corps.

Bulletins, III. When beads count

As far as
historians can
determine, bulletins
are not an article of faith.
Unless you count the Lutheran
women in Michigan who recycle
bulletins by making bulletin beads
and string necklaces out of them, and
that way people could wear their
bulletins when they go out
to coffee after church.
But those are
exceptions
to the
bulletin
rule.

Bulletin, IV. Evangel of the world

When you stop and think
about it, bulletins tell you
what you already know:
Jesus saves sinners
and the parish council meets.
So why the hymn numbers
[which are posted anyway]
and scripture readings
[which are announced]
or name the sermon
as if what the preacher talked about
had anything at all
to do with the title.
Give us something
really interesting
like God
really does
remake the world
and wants you
to have a go
at it too.
Other than that,
bulletins are dry
as dust and won't get
you into heaven, or patch
things up when you're your
kids have left home for the
last time three days in a row.
So what I want to know
is what's the fuss
about the bulletins?

Tom Decker

This guy

sees my windshield sticker
and up and tells me
that he was a prisoner of war
from viet nam, yessir he says
I was in the hanoi hilton
but didn't see too many
vietnamese mostly
russians and cubans
who came there to
question us and
then they'd beat us.
He said he now lives
in patagonia with his friend
who makes wooden flutes
to sell to tourists
at the craft shows
and he says that they
do okay, and I decided
that he was probably
a fake because most ex-pows
don't talk about it,
least ways not the first time.
besides that he said
he was a command warrant,
and I don't think he knows what
he's talking about, and he didn't
recognize the rank on my windshield.

The Intervention Rag

Hey man! Hey, lady!
This class will pass!
It is a gas!
It's the intervention rag;
the prevention jag!

Suicide.
's what we're talkin' about
'bout keepin' a life,
'bout makin' up with the wife,
'bout bein' a man,
'bout bein' a lady,
'bout doin' things right,
and not goin' crazy
in the middle of the night,
and bein' up tight,
when nothin' ain't' right,
and the only sound
which is goin' down
round and round,
round in the head,
is I'm better off dead!
Better off dead!
Better off dead!

No!
It's the crazy thinkin'
The stinkin' thinkin'
What's goin' around
In this town,

Getting people down,
And causin' em to frown'
Wantin' to drown it all
and end it all.

So this here is
The prevention word,
The intervention word,
That everybody's heard
About doin' it right
When things are up tight.

And we're sayin' to you:
No more drugs or glue,
    Goes for booze too,
No more bullets in the gun,
    Or takin in the sun,
No more shot-gun blast,
    A thing of the past,
No more slittin' the wrist,
No more ropes that twist,
No more lye down the throat,
No more drownin' out the boat,
No more takin' the leap,
No more dyin' in the sleep,
No more fallin' on a knife,
    To end the life
No more heavy use,
    Of that drug abuse,

No more goin' crazy,
In the middle of the night,
When nothin' ain't right,
And the only sound
goin' down,
round and round,
round in the head,
Is I'm better off dead!
Better off dead!
Better off dead!

No!
It's the crazy thinkin'
The stinkin' thinkin'

What's goin' around
In this town,
Getting people down,
and causin' em to frown'
wantin' to drown it all;
end it all.

Is the crazy thinkin'
The stinkin' thinkin'
'bout suicide!
Ain't no way to live;
ain't no way to die!
Gotta give life a try!
Give God a try,
Rather live than die!

So this little talk,
And this little walk,
Is to make you think,
'n erase the stink
of suicidal thoughts,
and getting' down,
depressed and low
with nowhere to go,
thinkin' no one'll know,

So put away the knife,
And save a life.
Put away the rope,
And have a little hope.
Put away the gun,
And have some fun.
Put away the booze,
You gotta lot to lose.
Put away the stuff,
Yeah, life's a little rough,

But death is the end,
Death is the end,
When there ain't no more
when you shut that door,
Bang! That's it!
Bang! That's it!

So do your bit
For suicide prevention,
And make an intervention.

Where will it end?
With you, my friend!
Where will it end?
With you, my friend!
So heed the word
you now have heard.

So take the dare,
And begin to care.
Grow a little bolder,
Try lovin' the soldier,
Let 'em grow a whole lot older.

So go ahead, take the time!
It don't cost a dime!

Remember this tune
the next full moon:
's what we're talkin' about
's 'bout savin' a life
'bout being a man,
'bout being a lady,
'bout doin' things right,
and not goin' crazy.

It's the intervention rag,
The prevention jag!

And
    it's
        all
            right!

Tom Decker

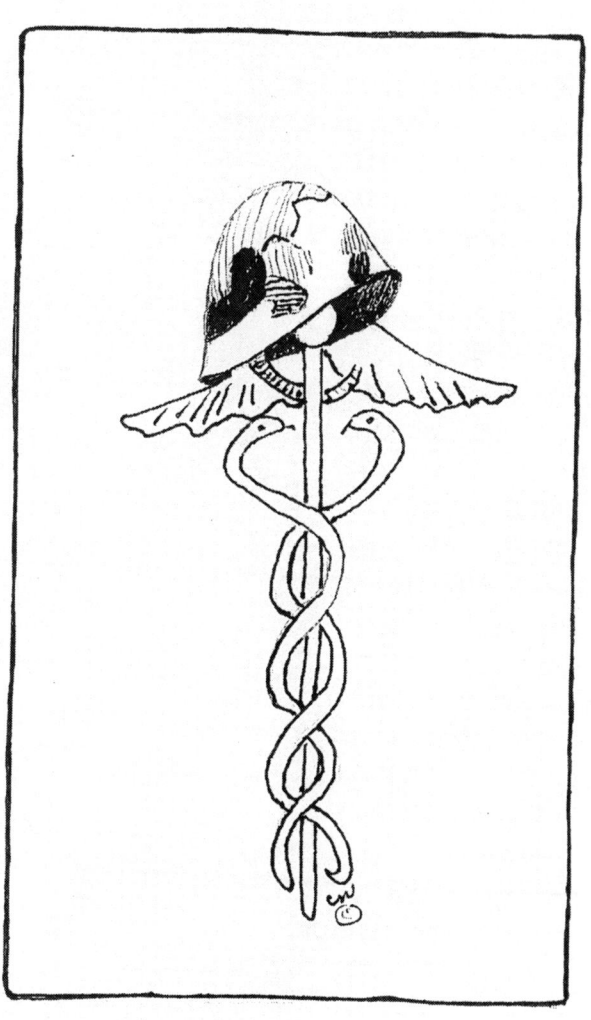

The salvation beat!

Okay, now! Preacher's my name
And salvation's the game.
Let the Word be preached
And lost souls reached.
Bring on the sinners,
Bad ones and beginners.

Stand 'em in the aisles,
Let 'em lose their wiles,
Get the backfield in motion
With the Gospel commotion,

Stand 'em up, Rev.,
And get 'em on down
Put a smile on the face
Instead of that frown.

Let the Word loose!
Let the Word loose!
'Cause when the Word is loose,
There ain't no use,
To be sweatin' and a jivin'
Not knowing what's drivin'
This old world around,
And it keeps going 'round.

Don'tcha know, sister;
Don'tcha know, mister?
The world's the Lord's place!
You can see his face.
You can see his grace,
It's in every place,.
It's in what He made,
It's in what He's done,
By giving us the Son,
By giving us the Son.

So today's the day,
It's the Lord's day!
Pay attention now, ya'll
When you hear the call,
It's the Lord who's a comin'
You can hear the drummin'

I say, it's the Lord who's comin'
You can hear the drummin'
Of the Gospel beat,
Marchin in the street
So get on board,
Get right with the Lord!

Put away the shame,
Don't play that game!
Put away the fear,
For the Lord is here!

Com on, sis! Come on, bud!
Come on down,
Get right with the blood!
You can see it comin'
You can hear the drummin'
The Lord's in town,
And he's goin' aroun'
Bringin' peace to the town!
His salvation is free,
It includes you and me!
So be sweet on your brother,
Your sister too.
Salvation's here; it's what to do!

Don'tcha know,
It's the Lord who's a comin'
You can hear the drummin'
Of the gospel beat,
Marching in the street
And oh, ain't it sweet?

Today's the Lord's day,
The Lord's day!

So pay attention, ya'll
When you hear the call,
It's the Lord who's a comin'
You can hear the drummin'

Say, it's the Lord who's comin'
You can hear the drummin'

Of the Gospel Beat,
Marching in the street,

So get on board,
Get right with the Lord!

Say, now's the time!
Yeah!

The bread of life

The fathers
had it wrong
when they said
fasting was an exercise
in discipline. From what
I can tell after one day of going
without cheese and milk, and then
blowing it completely with a turkey
pastrami sandwich at lunch is that
fasting marks not discipline but
failure, proof positive that we
need the Lord's help in all
things, especially in
satisfying the
hunger of
the world.

Big Appetite

O Lord,
We could have met at Burger King
Or McDonald's
Or even at the Windermere
Or gone to Bisbee to the Copper Queen,
Or we could have gone to
Ivey's or Little Bits,

And had a great breakfast
Of eggs, and biscuits & potatoes
And ham or even huevos rancheros

But we are meeting here to do our best
Not for food but for people
That they might fly and eat
And be with loved ones

So take care of unexpected needs.
And, O Lord, bless our eating here today
When we take the whole Army family to
    breakfast;
And know that when you are present,
There is always more than enough.
So bless us, the Army,
And all those who do their bit
That others may escape
    The clutches of dire necessity.

Amen.

Army Emergency Relief Fund Drive
Kickoff Breakfast

Sometimes

I tell
my friends
that I've got a
couple of icons
and then I have to
explain that they are
real icons and not the
kind that comes with micro-
soft word. I'd really like to
explain that they help me
pray but I never get that
far, because why would
somebody raised in
Sunday school pray
to a saint? I'd like
to say more, but
I'm not sure
that it'd
matter.

Chapter 9

They can't do this to me!
The soldier said,
He spoke roughly, assured,
But his hands held his head.

They're putting me out!
They're letting me go.
They say I'm not fit,
And why I don't know.

I've polished my boots.
And I've shined my brass.
I've done all my duty,
Now I'm out on my ass.

My wife…they don't care.
My kids,…they don't know.
If they go through with this,
Where will I go?

I've been to the JAG,
He said see the IG.
I went to the chaplain,
He just listened to me.

I just smoked one joint,
It was on Christmas Day.
God, it was good stuff,
Now there's hell to pay.

I guess I slipped up.
What else can I say?
I guess this is it.
There's no other way.

Sunnive and Jon

said that in Germany
most of the theology
students get their
education but never
get a church,
They thought it was odd
that in America it's just
the opposite.

Sunnive and Jon II

I said well, why not join
the U. S. Army and be
a chaplain, and you
can move when your
congregation moves
to Bosnia
or Kosovo
or Saudi
or Kuwait
or Korea
or to places where
they speak Spanish,
and they said ummhmmm
that was an interesting
but Africa was calling
and they'd pretty much
decided to spend
their lives there
on a mission
for Jesus.
So I guess that
Jesus hadn't
called them
for this
Army.

Baseball's Opener

We pray, O Lord, and we don't need a reason,
We pray for You to bless this base ball
    season!

Make it a gee-whiz time, a winning season for
    all!
We pray for batters to just hit the ball.

Help players and bats to do their best!
Help coaches and parents to meet the test.

Help pitchers to throw such fast strikes
That the opposing team yells, Yikes!

Help batters to hit even thrown balls,
And help umpires to watch their calls.

Help infielders to snag hot grounders,
And help outfielders to pull down rounders.

Help the infield to play it tight,
So the outfield can play it right.

Help us all, young and old,
To play baseball like we're told.

Help us all to not drop the ball,
To play it safe, or not play at all.

Help parents and coaches to keep a sense of humor,
And then this ball season will be a real boomer.

Remind us, O Lord, that it's just a game,
But let us win once in a while if it's all the same.

Tom Decker

No black eye for America

The biggest thing last week
was when 15 soldiers and two civilians
were ceremonied out to Macedonia
to fly the UAVs* for the Army.

Families came from near and far to see
their sons and daughters before they took off,
while the generals and colonels made
   speeches
about what a great job
they were doing for the Army,

and when they lined up everybody to give
   them
a yellow flower--because by now it's an Army
   tradition--
this one guy went up when they called his
   name,
with his mother and his lady on each arm,

and he had two black eyes
and a grin from ear to ear

The guy standing next to me
said that he got them in Tucson
when somebody insulted his lady;
but said he could see good enough
to fly a UAV.

[*UAV is an unmanned aerial vehicle used for surveillance work on the battlefield]

Dry heat

The commanding general called some
    meeting
on how we could improve the army and do
things better for the customer, and every-
body thought they knew who it was, but
they couldn't fix the air conditioning
even though they kept checking the
thermostat and sending out for a
sergeant who was supposed
to know how to do it,
so we sat there and
sweltered
with no windows,
and nobody said anything,
and you couldn't tell if it was
the onions left over from lunch
or some unsuspecting b.o. that was
making the room a bit close, so we
really didn't get a lot done for the Army.

Keepers of the Spirit

Ministry teams
Keep the spirit
during deployments
and training exercisxes
when they're separated
--yes, for all kinds of reasons!
when they're TDY
and in school
when they're newlyweds
and when marriage is old hat
when they're bearing
and rearing children
when the finances are tight
and they don't know why
when they're angry
and hurting
when they're sick or wounded
and there's no meaning to life
when they're disconnected
and want to get together again
and, oh yes, when they want to celebrate
their life
    with God!

You are sleeping

You
are sleeping
and you are Georgia
painting, painting, painting
petals of a desert blossom
and the sky becomes so very large .

You
are sleeping,
and you are Georgia,
and your clouds float high
over the New Mexico Pedernales

You
Are sleeping,
And you are Georgia,
and how dare I question
what keeps our love alive?

A Prayer for the Army's Birthday
June 14 1775

We remember, O Lord,
on this Anniversary of the United States Army,
the marches of our Army,

Training marches on parade field
    and bivouac areas,
dusty columns of horse cavalry
    and motor vehicles,
the turbulence of helicopters on assault,
forced marches to meet the enemy,
the quick march into battle,
the silent marches of lonely patrols,
the death march of the prisoners of war,
the lonely marches of the missing in action,
and a grateful nation on parade
at the end of conflict
    for the joyous return of soldiers
        to home and family.

Quicken our step, O Lord,
As we fall into this great formation
of our Army past & present,
And straighten our ranks for the future.

Deliver our ranks
from dressing on mediocrity
and the pride of self-service,

Keep this Army in step
for the long march of freedom.
Keep us in time to the drum beat
   of duty, honor, and country.

Amen.

About the Author

Tom Decker, almost a native of Idaho and a former smokejumper, answered the call to study for the ministry while yet in high school. Upon graduation and ordination in 1969 from Concordia Seminary in St Louis, the military chaplaincy beckoned—and with wife's urging—he traded a clerical collar for a National Guard military uniform less than a year into his first parish. Several years of weekend guard drills and summer camps convinced the young pastor that he should seek full-time service which came in 1975. For the next 27 years, his service as a chaplain tied God's love to men and women in uniform. Additionally the military gave him the ongoing challenge of bringing his spirituality into focus with the demands of the military's mission to be the nation's first line of defense. In the old Cold War setting, he served in the Army's 1st, 2nd, 4th, and 8th infantry divisions with stateside and overseas assignments at battalion, brigade, and division level. A graduate of the U. S. Army War College, he attained the rank of Colonel and was assigned in Korea as the senior chaplain in the military's medical command. Upon returning to the states, he became the Installation Staff Chaplain at Fort Huachuca, Arizona, a historic post in southeastern Arizona. Throughout Decker's career, he was not only a religious leader and counselor but also a keen observer of how darkness becoming light plays out in the lives of those who are touched with God's great love. The retired chaplain and pastor is married to Janice

Debandt Decker of Birmingham, Michigan; they have four children and four grandchildren. Upon retirement from the military in 2002, Decker served a small Lutheran urban congregation in Long Beach, CA until his retirement in 2008.